Dear Parent:
Your child's love of reading starts here!

Every child learns to read in a different way and at his or her own speed. Some go back and forth between reading levels and read favorite books again and again. Others read through each level in order. You can help your young reader improve and become more confident by encouraging his or her own interests and abilities. From books your child reads with you to the first books he or she reads alone, there are I Can Read Books for every stage of reading:

SHARED READING
Basic language, word repetition, and whimsical illustrations, ideal for sharing with your emergent reader

BEGINNING READING
Short sentences, familiar words, and simple concepts for children eager to read on their own

READING WITH HELP
Engaging stories, longer sentences, and language play for developing readers

READING ALONE
Complex plots, challenging vocabulary, and high-interest topics for the independent r~~der

ADVANCED RE~
Short paragraphs, ch
for the perfect bridg

I Can Read Books have introduced children to the joy of reading since 1957. Featuring award-winning authors and illustrators and a fabulous cast of beloved characters, I Can Read Books set the standard for beginning readers.

A lifetime of discovery begins with the magical words "I Can Read!"

Visit www.icanread.com for information
on enriching your child's reading experience.

In memory of Dr. Joel Silidker
—L.D.

"To all the amazing doctors and nurses I know,
who give so much of themselves every day of the year.
Your passion and dedication is admirable.
Thank you for all that you do!"
—Catalina Echeverri

I Can Read Book® is a trademark of HarperCollins Publishers.

I Want to Be a Doctor. Copyright © 2018 by HarperCollins Publishers. All rights reserved. Manufactured in U.S.A.
No part of this book may be used or reproduced in any manner whatsoever without written permission except in the case of
brief quotations embodied in critical articles and reviews. For information address HarperCollins Children's Books,
a division of HarperCollins Publishers, 195 Broadway, New York, NY 10007.
www.icanread.com

Library of Congress Control Number: 2016949890
ISBN 978-0-06-243241-4 (trade bdg.) — ISBN 978-0-06-243240-7 (pbk.)

Typography by Jeff Shake
20 LSCC 10 ❖ First Edition

I Can Read!

BEGINNING
1
READING

I Want to Be a Doctor

by Laura Driscoll

illustrated by Catalina Echeverri

HARPER
An Imprint of HarperCollinsPublishers

We are at the hospital—
my mom and dad,
my brother, Jack, and me.

Jack is not so happy.

His foot hurts a lot.

I saw the whole thing.

Jack flew off the top bunk.

Maybe he forgot he can't fly.

Dad put ice on Jack's foot.

His foot is black and blue.

Mom thinks it could be broken.

So here we are

in the emergency room.

It is a busy place.

Some people are hurt.

Some are sick.

It is a good thing
doctors are here to help.

"I like to help people, too,"

I tell the doctor.

Her name is Dr. Tate.

"Maybe you will be

a doctor someday!" she says.

Dr. Tate looks at Jack's foot.

She touches it gently.

"Let's take an X-ray," she says.

"It will show us

if any bones are broken."

We go to another part
of the hospital.
An X-ray machine
takes a picture of Jack's foot.

A man comes to look at the X-ray.

"Are you a doctor, too?" I ask.

"Yes!" he says.

"I am Dr. Dean.

I read X-rays."

The doctor sees a small break
in one of Jack's bones.
So next we go to see Dr. Jones,
a bone doctor.

"There are doctors
just for bones?" I ask.

"Yes!" Dr. Jones says.

"Just like there are heart doctors, brain doctors, and skin doctors."

"Who did you see

to get those glasses?"

Dr. Jones asks.

"The eye doctor!" I say.

"What do you call
your tooth doctor?" Dr. Jones asks.
"The dentist!" I say.

"And who do you see
for checkups?" he asks.
"My regular doctor," I say.
"Oh! I get it.
She's a *kid* doctor!"

Mom and Jack

go into the exam room.

Dad and I decide to get a snack.

20

In the cafeteria,
we see lots of doctors and nurses
on their lunch breaks.
Dr. Tate is one of them.

"I used to think

there was only one kind of doctor,"

I tell Dr. Tate.

"But there are so many kinds!"

"What kind would you be?"

Dr. Tate asks.

I shrug.

"Well, would you like to meet

a few more?" she asks.

Dr. Tate takes us
around the hospital.
We meet Dr. Lu,
who is a baby doctor.
"I've always loved
working with little ones,"
Dr. Lu says.

Then we meet Dr. Kent.

He helps people walk again

after an injury.

"I really get to know

the people I treat," Dr. Kent says.

"Some of them I see every day."

We meet Dr. Lopez,

who works in a lab.

She does tests to see

what is making someone sick.

"You must like puzzles," I say.

"Yes," Dr. Lopez says.

"Our work is like solving mysteries."

I ask Dr. Tate

what she likes about

being an emergency room doctor.

"I meet so many people," she says.

"Every day is different.

And busy!"

Later we go find Mom and Jack.

Jack has on a special boot.

He needs to wear it

for a few weeks.

It will help his bone heal.

Jack can even walk with it!

He is feeling

so much better . . .

all thanks to doctors.

Meet the Doctors

Emergency room doctor
a doctor who works in the emergency room of the hospital

Radiologist
a doctor who reads X-rays

Orthopedist
a doctor who helps to fix bones

Neonatologist
a doctor who helps newborn babies

Physical therapist
a doctor who helps patients do exercises so they can heal and move better after they've hurt themselves

Pathologist
a doctor who does tests in a laboratory to figure out what is making someone sick

Dentist
a doctor who takes care of teeth

Ophthalmologist
an eye doctor

Pediatrician
a doctor for children